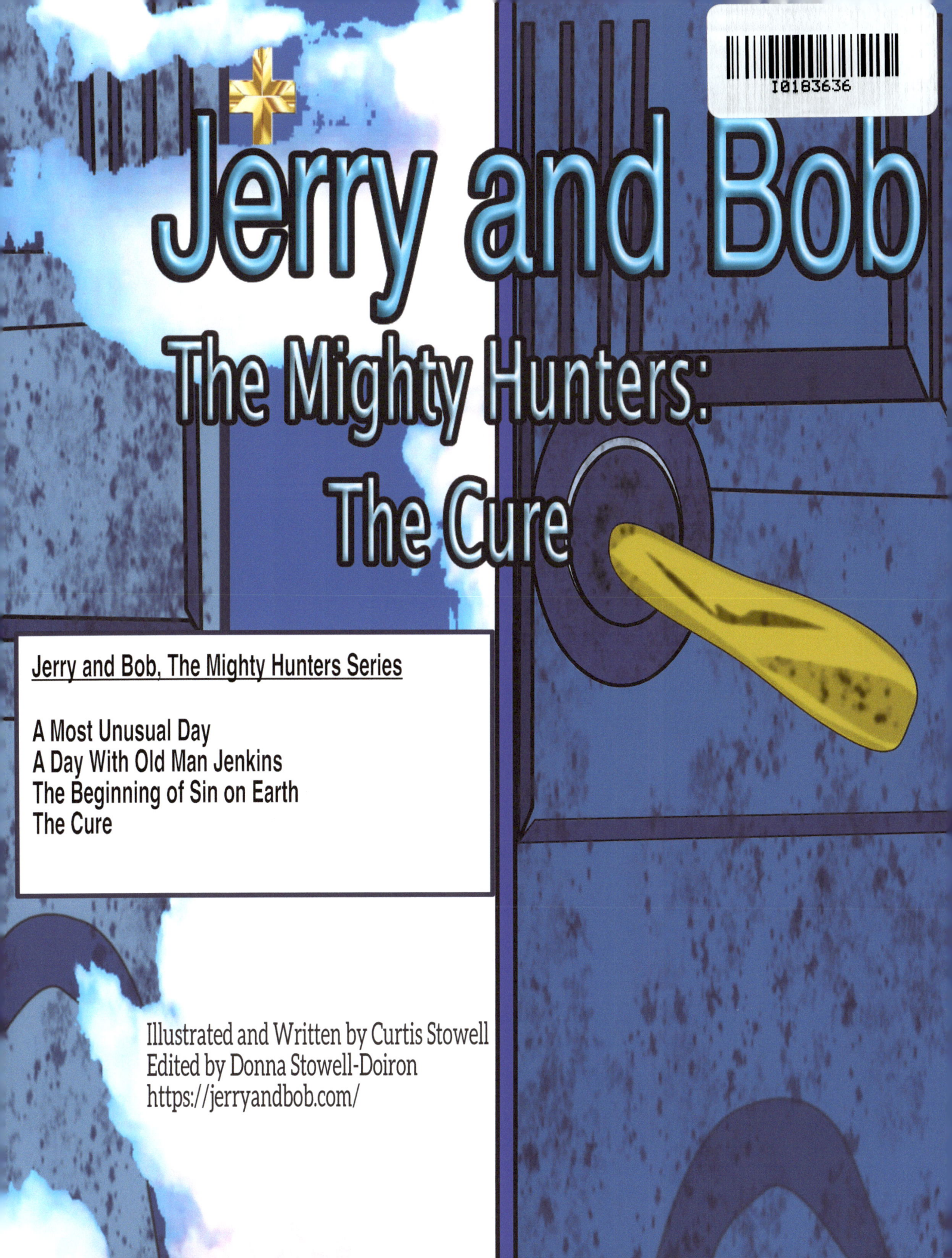

Jerry and Bob
The Mighty Hunters: The Cure

Jerry and Bob, The Mighty Hunters Series

A Most Unusual Day
A Day With Old Man Jenkins
The Beginning of Sin on Earth
The Cure

Illustrated and Written by Curtis Stowell
Edited by Donna Stowell-Doiron
https://jerryandbob.com/

Jerry and Bob

The Mighty Hunters:

The Beginning of Sin on Earth

Book 3 of the "Jerry and Bob: The Mighty Hunters" series.

Copyright © 2025 Curtis Stowell

All rights reserved. No part of this publication may be reproduced, distributed, or transmitted in any form or by any means, including photocopying, recording, or other electronic or mechanical methods, without the prior written permission of the publisher.

This is a work of fiction. Any resemblance to actual events or persons, living or dead, is entirely coincidental.

ISBN: 978-1-956246-09-4

Published by Curtis Stowell

Printed by Kindle Direct Publisher in the United States of America.

Jerry and Bob, the Mighty Hunters:
The Beginning of Sin on Earth

Book 3, Jerry will learn about Jesus Christ. Bob will tell about a website that he thinks pertains to Jerry and God. Satan, Adam and Eve, and the cause of Sin is explained. The Holy Ghost will be introduced.

The purpose of the "Jerry and Bob" series is to share the Bible in a fun way. To entertain, but also to do what Jesus had asked his disciples to do:

> "And he said unto them, Go ye into all the world, and preach the gospel to every creature"
> (Mk 16:15).

Jerry is ten years old and somewhat of a rascal and quite adventurous, but well behaved. His mother is the District Attorney of their home town and that could certainly be why.

Bob is also ten years old. His father is the head pastor of a small Christian church, so he knows a bit about God. He's not quite as curious or brave as Jerry. Bob would never try to bend a rule or take a shortcut, but he's still a boy.

It wouldn't be expected, but they are the best of friends and call themselves The Mighty Hunters. They're not sure, but they think they may need another one to join them, like the Three Musketeers.

This story is about Jerry and Bob, but the sole purpose of it is to teach children and adults about Jesus Christ.

For educational purposes, scriptures are shown at the bottom of certain pages. I hope you enjoy it.

Curtis Stowell

Page	About	Scriptures
4	Angels unseen	Heb 13:2
9	There is only one God	Isa 46:9
10	God is a fearful, but loving God	Eph 1:4, Deut 32:39
11	About God	1 Tim 2:5, Ex 34:14, Deut 4:24, Isa 44:6, Isa 43:11, Rev 1:8, Isa 42:8, Jn 10:30
12	The devil fears God	James 2:19
17	Born Again	Jn 3:3
19	Without Jesus you can do nothing	Jn 15:5
20	The unrighteous will not go to heaven	1 Cor 6:9-6:10
22	Forgiveness of Sin	Is 43:25, Heb 10:26-27, 31
23	Born Again	Jn 3:3
24	Roaring Lion	1 Pet 5:8
26	Apostle Paul was the chief sinner	1 Tim 1:15
29	Paul's meeting with Jesus	Acts 9:1-9
30	The Old Man is replaced	Eph 4:22-24
35	Apostle Paul Explains that Everyone Sins	Rom 3:23, Rom 7:14-25
40	Satan cast from heaven	Is 14:13-15
41	Hell was made for the devil	Matt 25:41
42	Narrow is the gate	Matt 7:13-14
43	The Trinity	1 Jn 5:7
46	Born Again	Jn 3:3
47	Jesus never sinned	2 Cor 5:21, 1 Pert 2:22
48	One man brings death, Jesus brings life	Rom 5:12 & 19
49	Only God and Jesus can forgive sin	Mark 2:7, 10

Jerry thinks he sees an angel so he and Bob slowly approach it.

Jerry is bothered by this "sin thing" because he doesn't understand it. He likes to solve problems, but this has him stumped. But Bob knows how to fix it.

"Remember the former things of old: for I am God, and there is none else; I am God, and there is none like me" (Isa 46:9).

"According as he hath chosen us in him before the foundation of the world, that we should be holy and without blame before him in love" (Eph 1:4).

"See now that I, even I, am he, and there is no god with me: I kill, and I make alive; I wound, and I heal: neither is there any that can deliver out of my hand" (Deut 32:39).

"I am Alpha and Omega, the beginning and the ending, saith the Lord, which is, and which was, and which is to come, the Almighty" (Rev 1:8).

"For *there is* one God, and one mediator between God and men, the man Christ Jesus" (1 Tim 2:5).

"Thou believest that there is one God; thou doest well: the devils also believe, and tremble" (James 2:19).

"For thou shalt worship no other god: for the LORD, whose name is Jealous, is a jealous God" (Ex 34:14).

"For the LORD thy God is a consuming fire, even a jealous God" (Deut 4:24).

"Thus saith the LORD the King of Israel, and his redeemer the LORD of hosts; I *am* the first, and I *am* the last; and beside me *there is* no God" (Isa 44:6).

"I, *even* I, *am* the LORD; and beside me *there is* no saviour" (Isa 43:11).

"I *am* the LORD: that *is* my name: and my glory will I not give to another, neither my praise to graven images" (Isa 42:8).

"I [Jesus] and *my* Father are one" (Jn 10:30).

"Thou believest that there is one God; thou doest well: the devils also believe, and tremble" (James 2:19).

"Jesus answered and said unto him, Verily, verily, I say unto thee, Except a man be born again, he cannot see the kingdom of God" (Jn 3:3).

"Know ye not that the unrighteous shall not inherit the kingdom of God? Be not deceived: neither fornicators, nor idolaters, nor adulterers, nor effeminate, nor abusers of themselves with mankind,

Nor thieves, nor covetous, nor drunkards, nor revilers, nor extortioners, shall inherit the kingdom of God." (Jn 15:5).

"I, even I, am he that blotteth out thy transgressions for mine own sake, and will not remember thy sins" (Is 43:25).

"For if we sin wilfully after that we have received the knowledge of the truth, there remaineth no more sacrifice for sins,

But a certain fearful looking for of judgment and fiery indignation, which shall devour the adversaries.

It is a fearful thing to fall into the hands of the living God. (Heb 10:26-27, 31).

You Must Be Born Again

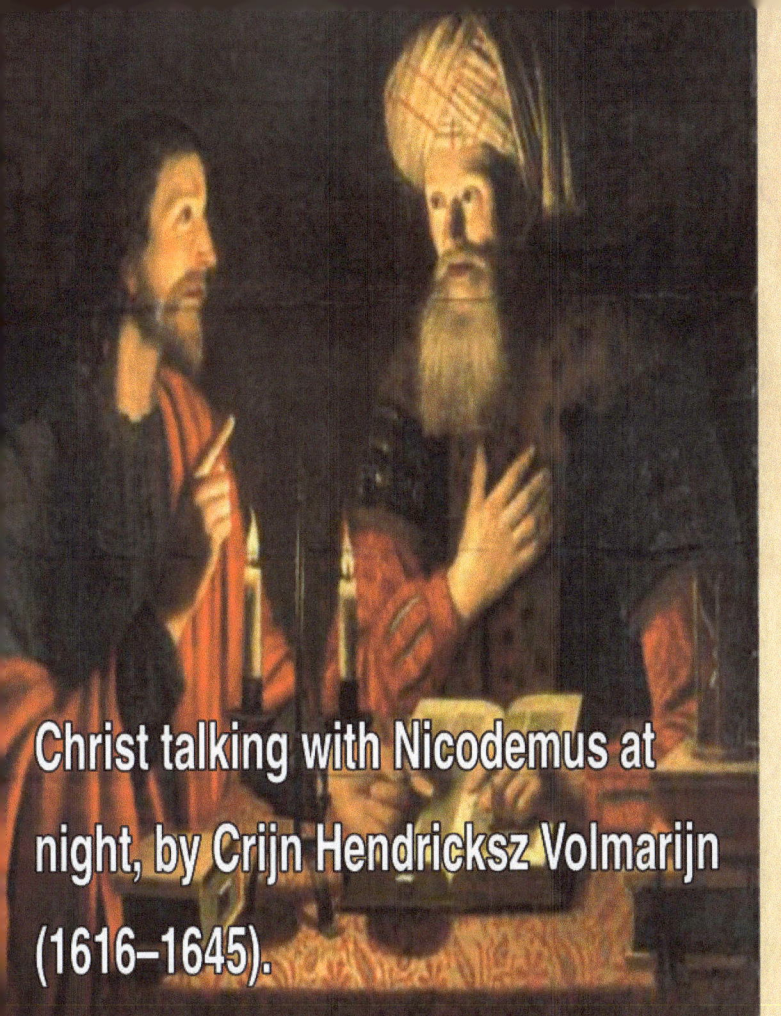

Christ talking with Nicodemus at night, by Crijn Hendricksz Volmarijn (1616–1645).

"There was a man of the Pharisees, named Nicodemus, a ruler of the Jews:

The same came to Jesus by night, and said unto him, Rabbi, we know that thou art a teacher come from God: for no man can do these miracles that thou doest, except God be with him.

Jesus answered and said unto him, Verily, verily, I say unto thee, Except a man be born again, he cannot see the kingdom of God.

Nicodemus saith unto him, How can a man be born when he is old? can he enter the second time into his mother's womb, and be born?

Jesus answered, Verily, verily, I say unto thee, Except a man be born of water and of the Spirit, he cannot enter into the kingdom of God.

That which is born of the flesh is flesh; and that which is born of the Spirit is spirit.

Marvel not that I said unto thee, Ye must be born again" (Jn 3:1-7).

"Be sober, be vigilant; because your adversary the devil, as a roaring lion, walketh about, seeking whom he may devour" (1 Pet 5:8).

Statue: The Apostle Paul
Engraving: P Folo after L Camia after B Thorwaldsen.
Contributors: Bertel Thorvaldsen (1770-1844); Leonardo Camià; Pietro Folo. Work ID: yxu5zuac.

The Colosseum is in the center of the city of Rome. The largest ancient amphitheater ever built, and still the largest standing in the world today. Built in 72 to 80 AD.

And Saul, yet breathing out threatenings and slaughter against the disciples of the Lord, went unto the high priest,

And desired of him letters to Damascus to the synagogues, that if he found any of this way, whether they were men or women, he might bring them bound unto Jerusalem.

And as he journeyed, he came near Damascus: and suddenly there shined round about him a light from heaven:

And he fell to the earth, and heard a voice saying unto him, Saul, Saul, why persecutest thou me?

And he said, Who art thou, Lord? And the Lord said, I am Jesus whom thou persecutest: it is hard for thee to kick against the pricks.

And he trembling and astonished said, Lord, what wilt thou have me to do? And the Lord said unto him, Arise, and go into the city, and it shall be told thee what thou must do.

And the men which journeyed with him stood speechless, hearing a voice, but seeing no man.

And Saul arose from the earth; and when his eyes were opened, he saw no man: but they led him by the hand, and brought him into Damascus.

"That ye put off concerning the former conversation the old man, which is corrupt according to the deceitful lusts;

And be renewed in the spirit of your mind;

And that ye put on the new man, which after God is created in righteousness and true holiness." (Eph 4:22-24).

The Apostle Paul Explains that All Have Sinned

"For all have sinned, and come short of the glory of God" (Rom 3:23).

"For we know that the law is spiritual: but I am carnal, sold under sin.

For that which I do I allow not: for what I would, that do I not; but what I hate, that do I.

If then I do that which I would not, I consent unto the law that it is good.

Now then it is no more I that do it, but sin that dwelleth in me.

For I know that in me (that is, in my flesh,) dwelleth no good thing: for to will is present with me; but how to perform that which is good I find not.

For the good that I would I do not: but the evil which I would not, that I do.

Now if I do that I would not, it is no more I that do it, but sin that dwelleth in me.

I find then a law, that, when I would do good, evil is present with me.

For I delight in the law of God after the inward man:

But I see another law in my members, warring against the law of my mind, and bringing me into captivity to the law of sin which is in my members.

O wretched man that I am! who shall deliver me from the body of this death?

I thank God through Jesus Christ our Lord. So then with the mind I myself serve the law of God; but with the flesh the law of sin" (Rom 7:14-24).

"Wherefore, as by one man sin entered into the world, and death by sin; and so death passed upon all men, for that all have sinned" (Rom 5:12).

"For as by one man's disobedience many were made sinners, so by the obedience of one shall many be made righteous" (Rom 5:19).

"Why doth this man thus speak blasphemies? who can forgive sins but God only?
"But that ye may know that the Son of man hath power on earth to forgive sins" (Mk 2:7 & 10).

Jerry is anxious to know more about Jesus and being Born Again.

Jerry and Bob are going to learn more about Old Man Jenkins, things that they never would have thought. They'll also learn something about Sally that they didn't know.

The Purple Pond is just around the corner, but they're not alone.

www.ingramcontent.com/pod-product-compliance
Lightning Source LLC
LaVergne TN
LVHW072126070426
835512LV00002B/19